Postcard Days

Postcard Days

Poems by Jennifer Soule

Cherry Grove Collections

© 2019 by Jennifer Soule

Published by Cherry Grove Collections

P.O. Box 541106

Cincinnati, OH 45254-1106

ISBN: 9781625493293

Poetry Editor: Kevin Walzer

Business Editor: Lori Jareo

Visit us on the web at www.cherry-grove.com

Contents

Happy Haiku Day 7
Morning Circle 9
Haiku Prayer 10
Blizzard Birthday January 12 11
Winter Woman 12
Prayer for June 14
August Ends 15
"Charm City" 16
Washington, DC: Light and Dark 18
Cherry Blossom Time Over Years 20
A Time for Herons 21
Southern Exposure 22
Sound Bites 23
Green Tea, with Camellia and Cardinal 24
Haiku prayers 27
Quality of Life 32

Happy Haiku Day

Often times we remember and write of the big days in our lives—graduations, journeys, weddings, births, deaths, and first book publications. And though we enjoy them, we sometimes forget the smaller postcard days.

One such day occurs for me in the spring of '99. My first haiku are accepted for publication in the journal *Modern Haiku*. For at least two years I have been sending off haiku to Robert Spiess in Madison, Wisconsin. Even when I forget the SASE, he responds promptly with lovely handwritten haiku-like notes and gentle suggestions to keep trying—"very close." He is usually so pleasant that these do not feel like the usual rejection notices: "Thank you for your submission, but this does not meet the needs of our publication at this time."

And then one May day at the end of the academic year it arrives. Two of my haiku have been accepted! The standard payment is enclosed—one dollar per haiku. Real money in the mail. For poetry.

I immediately run out of my house and down to my friend Linda's—only two blocks away. I burst through the door like a kid just home from school and start jumping up and down. I scream, "*Modern Haiku* accepted my haiku!" Linda, always the ebullient one, also begins jumping up and down and screaming like we are teenage girls at a rock concert. On one of the jumps I notice. She is not alone. Her friend Gregg—the Harvard educated lawyer—is visiting. This is not the type of guy who would be given to jumping up and down about much of anything—certainly not haiku. But he just smiles and I am excited enough that I do not feel the need to faint from embarrassment. I am over 50. This is important to me. So here they are:

April rain—
their newly planted maple
strung with Christmas lights

cherry blossom time
Holocaust Museum hidden
in pink/white softness

And just this week I read in *Poetry* a review of Hayden Carruth's poetry book, *Doctor Jazz*. The review begins with his haiku:

Basho, you made
     a living writing haiku?
          Wow! Way to go, man.

    It reminds me how much I love this small verse form and that once I got paid for a haiku even if I could never make a living at it. And so this Monday is another postcard happy moment.

light snow falling
calves grow heavy in mother's bellies
South Dakota March

Morning Circle

The moon setting in the west,
coyotes howling in the south,
a gold sun rising in the east,
lightning flashing in the north,
October morning softly circles.

Haiku Prayer

haiku
breathe me
home

on the Great Plains—
earth deep as the ocean
sky even wider

November evening
snow sky arrives—
lights turn on early

Blizzard Birthday January 12

As I turn 54
this cold foggy day
the bushes burn with hoarfrost.

This date in 1888
the Children's Blizzard
swept our end of South Dakota.

112 little ones
on their way home from school
did not arrive.

No storm advisories, Doppler.
No school buses. No paved roads.
And 54 was older, then.

Winter Woman

It's snowing lightly on the Black Hills. A gentle snow like soft Irish rain. And it's cold. A good day to stay in with chicken soup and Gypsy Cold Cure tea as I feel a cold coming on. But a woman born of winter, I can enjoy the season and endure.

Endurance and survival were my first early woman lessons. January—the coldest month. Anniversary of the Children's Blizzard. At only five pounds, I was swaddled and held close by my Mom. I learned there are warm places in cold, harsh times.

As a woman who had to love winter, I needed to discover its secrets. To love the quiet, slowed-down time of the year. The season of solitude. A time all women need to nourish the Self. I was lucky to learn this early. Still, at times I forget. But when the snow falls, I'm nudged to light candles on the dark day, build a fire, and make hot chocolate with marshmallows. Time to remember those early girl lessons.

Sunday snow
white on ponderosa pines—
quiet woman's day

winter snowscape
trees sparkle with frozen fog
steam from hogs too

Epiphany
the Christmas cookies
taste stale

dusk—
deer in snow
staring at me

Prayer for June

Let less happen in the realm
of extremes this summer
and make it as ordinary
as peonies opened to pink
by tiny ants.
July moon rise
fireflies come out to play
radio towers blink

August Ends

change moon
busy fullness
humming birds on the move,
doves coo and lovers good-bye
summer over

"Charm City"

One of the many misunderstandings about Baltimore is how it obtained the nickname of "charm city." It was an advertising campaign that did not quite capture the imagination of everyone and fell short of the Mayor's desire to upgrade the city image. It had nothing to do with the irascible H.L. Mencken who would have been appalled and was dead in the '70s but I was there and the irony of it "charmed" me. It probably would have charmed the queen of etiquette born there in 1872. She considered charm important in etiquette.

all lined up—
white marble stoops
brick row houses

cinnamon and garlic
McCormick spice company—
ahh…

As a young student, I had an adventurous time living above the Peabody Bookshop—one time speakeasy. Walking down Charles Street to the University of Maryland. The Harbor, the famous Block of Blaze Starr fame, and Fell's Point. I have some fond memories of a city quite unappreciated even if Babe Ruth had a house there. And Billie Holiday and Frank O'Hara also began life here. Edgar Allen Poe is still here.

Baltimore boasts
oyster bars, vegetable stands—
Lexington market

a single rose
and Edgar Allen Poe's grave—
Baltimore

Baltimore
And street vendors' horse drawn carts
bells jingle   horns honk

Washington, DC: Light and Dark

Washington, DC has been in and out of my life like a lover who keeps turning up. My first job after high school was here. I was protester in '60s movements here. Years later I lived within driving distance and frequented it for urban/cultural fixes. Like many cities, poverty and affluence live side by side as uneasy neighbors. The marble capitol building and the National Gallery of Art with the waterfall wall and painted treasures—are only blocks from the 14th Street prostitute and drug traffic.

Georgia O'Keeffe's sky—
downtown Washington, DC
crack cocaine on streets

When I taught in West Virginia I used to take my students to the homeless shelter kitchen, So Others Might Eat (SOME) to serve lunch. They were frightened while walking the several blocks from Union Station with its upscale boutiques out to the streets littered with liquor bottles and curb trash. After lunch we went to Senator Byrd's office to talk policy and he played the fiddle.

steam rises from grate
a woman sleeping on
Constitution Avenue

This city of laws and democracy capital is a magnet for protests. I remember the Poor People's march in 1968 with its tent city. I was there for my friend Kathy's wedding, but went to the march. The groom retrieved me from the Washington Monument grounds to have my hair curled for the wedding at Andrews Air Force Base. The poverty lasted. The marriage did not. Two years later I was tear-gassed during an antiwar demonstration—in front of the Justice Department.

cold November day—
students file past White House   stop
say name of soldier

It is the home of my favorite museum—The National Museum of Women in the Arts. The book art exhibits are a treat for me. As a book lover, I like to see the book developed as a work of art that tells a story. I own two of the works. One is colorful scenes of a tornado from an artist's view. Another, a circle of black and white photos on white paper: a visual memoir with words. As delicious as high tea at the elegant Hay-Adams Hotel on Lafayette Square.

jasmine tea
hot scones with thick cream—
immigrant waiters

But my all-time favorite memory of Washington, DC is cherry blossom time. One March visit to the Tidal Basin during the peak bloom was a haiku visit. After my mom and I walked around the pool of water ringed with trees of pink, I sat on a bench and wrote haiku. It was a peak experience. And the following haiku was subsequently published in *Modern Haiku*.

Washington, DC
the cars covered
in cherry blossoms

Cherry Blossom Time Over Years

At eighteen, on my own in Washington, I marveled
at the delicate pink blossoms surrounding
the Tidal Basin, so exotic for a prairie girl.

During my college professor years
cherry blossom viewing was an annual
jaunt from Shepherdstown, West Virginia

Older now, on a recent visit in late spring,
I appreciate more those gnarled trunks
after the peak of fickle princess pink.

A Time for Herons

Like many mental health professionals and academics, my husband and I take off the first few weeks of August. No one should work in this month of heat that wears heavy like a raccoon overcoat.

We drift about on our Pacific Seacraft sailboat on the Chesapeake Bay in Oxford, Maryland. Read escape literature. Feed the beautiful hissing swans.

We decide to take a voyage south to Smith Island. It is an island that was settled in the 1600s by the English. Their descendants never left. Just stayed, intermarried, and died here as the world moved centuries ahead of them. Now the civilized escape to Smith Island for quiet, seafood and opportunity to hear authentic Elizabethan accent. We sail in to the only pier late in the afternoon. Relief of tying the lines around pilings. Sigh. Wind no longer master.

But the best is waiting above us. After the all-you-can-eat seafood meal of big blue crabs, corn fritters, and fried oysters, we board our boat to watch the sunset. Then racket overhead. We are docked next to a heron rookery. Nests big as small haystacks flutter and shriek with young great blue herons. Heron already the size of pterodactyls want their dinner. Parents are busy bringing in blue fish carry-out. We watch until the sunset fades summer red on the Bay. For years I dream of big birds on an island that resists time with the sun rising on small white grave stones of people who knew only this hidden home.

sky
water
heron time

Southern Exposure

      Deeply rooted in the Great Plains/Prairie I felt secure enough to branch out and was eager to do so. Having no experience with the water other than the Big Sioux until I met my husband, it swallowed me. I loved our time the water—sailing, excursion down the Intracoastal Waterway, and finally living in the Keys on the boat. But we also lived in Alabama and Florida on land for a while. On land or on water. Action surrounds me. I take pleasure in just being with places as I come to know them in various seasons and activities of humans and other animals. Curiosity leads me to explore the places I live. The history, culture, foods, people, and natural resources enthrall and capture my imagination.

Sound Bites

Alabama sounds
like butter melting
on warm cornbread.
The words are meant
for tasting: Tuscaloosa,
Talladega, Loachapoka,
Opelika, Chattahoochee—
appetizers for a feast of sounds
to roll around the tongue
        and dip into poems.

Green Tea, with Camellia and Cardinal

This poem will not take the top
off your head. It is an insignificant
little quotidian poem picking
fresh parsley in February for dinner
in Alabama after a brief cold snap
and deadly tornados. It's a camellia
blowing pink kisses from a glass bowl.
It's air all moist and sexy whispering
Spring soon. It's a cardinal splishsplashing
in a bath after a drought, while
the gray mockingbird waits in line.
It's miso soup with sesame crackers
or a cup of green tea with a good friend.
Simple tastes of color and warmth.

small shy heron
lost in shadow of Great Blue...
his elegant striped vest

Halloween rose
won't give up ghost
cold as witch's tit

gray cat
scampers though yellow leaves
November crunches

gulls noisy
mating calls permeate marina—-
exhibitionists

love bugs...
lawn quivers alive
as May flies mate

rainy morn
frogs sing world
awake

white fence...
four blue birds grumble
at the rain

Valentine's Day—
we buy a red
microwave

after yoga class
bright September morning
I step in dog shit

Sunday afternoon
cooler than it's been
October silence

haiku like dreams
record at once
or lose forever

first patio tomato—
tasty mouthful meal
for the squirrel

cardinal on deck
eyeing empty birdbath—
looks to me
I get up to do his bidding
he strolls in with red towel

Haiku prayers

haiku
breathe me
whole

pelican swallows
whole meal in one gulp—
efficient takeout

barracuda
in shade of dock
quiet danger

wind howls today
an abandoned woman
somewhere…

Sunday morning
great blue heron on rooftop—
a different view

walking across Seven Mile Bridge—
ocean and Gulf meet below—
the hiss of high voltage lines

gulls call outside
inside the boat
I peck computer keys

heavy June rainstorm—
pelican opens mouth wide
takes a long drink

clouds hang over mangroves
I pause in journal writing—
blue patches appear

blue sky
white clouds
gentle breeze
enough

Monarch butterflies
circle garden in quiet flutters
plane soars overhead

fish market—
gulls and shoppers
snap up catch-of-the-day

news brief—
Turtle Hospital now accepting
dolphins, eagles

lazy summer
watching the lizards play
in shade

summer solstice
lingering over dinner
our anniversary

summer solstice
osprey hunts
late dinner

vase of red roses
stands on a bridge—
what anniversary?

two seagulls shrieking
together on same piling—
spring mating ritual

full orange moon rises
behind red radio towers—
quickly soars above

great white heron
emerald mangroves—
man fishes at dock

clouds form winter quilt
over tropical island—
storm thundering through

Monday morning
fast food wrappers next to seagrass
on fishing pier

total lunar eclipse
moon becomes orange/copper ball—
winter night fire

on walk with husband—
turtle doves in mating dance
March winds blowing

in resort towns
restaurants come and go
along with tourists

vacation eateries
have short lives
tourists fickle lovers

morning tableau—
two fishermen— one portly
one slender heron

early April morn
great white heron at water's edge—
grocery cart, too

prank highway sign
"Bridge freezes in winter"—
in the Florida Keys

at the grocery store—
among the peppers and carrots—
errant redstart sings

Quality of Life

A ruby-throated humming bird
ravages red from every flower.

I inhale bruschetta and crème brulee
with Geri as emerald waves kiss kids.

Pelicans fish off the Bay Bridge,
a piling stands reserved for each.

I steal lilacs and childhood memories
from the house with the chartreuse door.

Mockingbirds outside my window
tease me about my poetry.

The five-year-old girl devours
an ice cream cone with her whole body.

I recall stomping grapes into wine
that explodes all over Upper Michigan.

Blues on Pensacola beach
jam under the clam shell every Tuesday.

I dream flocks of snow geese in sloppy V's
above the Missouri River.

Summer escapes with no hurricanes
but grabs a bowl of fresh Maine blueberries.

No checkout lines at Safeway abduct
my Saturday shopping for artichokes.

Acknowledgements

Thanks to the editors of the following publications in which some of the poems in this collection appeared previously, albeit sometimes in different versions or with different titles. My sincere apologies for any omissions.

Modern Haiku "April rain, "cherry blossom time", "Heron Time"
Pasque Petals "Morning Circle"
Scurfpea "Winter Woman"

I also want to thank my good friends and family, too numerous to mention, who have been faithful supporters, reading and editing poems over the years while sharing many postcard days and other special times. Especially, my husband Brad—-first and last reader.

I am also grateful for the helpful technical assistance, editing, and design work of Kevin Walzer and Lori Jareo at WordTech for Cherry Grove Collections.

Jennifer Soule's poems have appeared in *South Dakota Review*, *The Sow's Ear Poetry Review* and *Modern Haiku*, among others including various anthologies. *Finishing Line Press* published her first chapbook, *Hiawatha Asylum for Insane Indians*. She has been a community organizer, clinical social worker and professor in various parts of the country. A South Dakota native, she returned to Sioux Falls (hometown) with her husband Brad. As a professor emerita (social work) with an MFA in creative writing, she now has time to combine her varied interests and devote more time to writing. Her passion for place and language continue to be well nurtured in South Dakota.

Made in the USA
Lexington, KY
22 November 2019